C000096547

The Big Picnic

Explorer Challenge
Who eats this sandwich?

OXFORD
UNIVERSITY PRESS

Biff and Chip had a big bag.

Mum put a rug on the sand.

Dad had a dish of chicken.

"Yum! A picnic in the sun," said Kipper.

Mum had a big tub of salad.
"Tuck in," she said.

Chip was full up.

Biff was full up.

Kipper was full up, too.

13

"Shall I put this back in the bag?" said Dad.

"Um," said Chip.
"Well," said Biff.

Dad had a fantastic cake.

"We are not *that* full," said Kipper.

Retell the Story

Look at the pictures and retell the story in your own words.

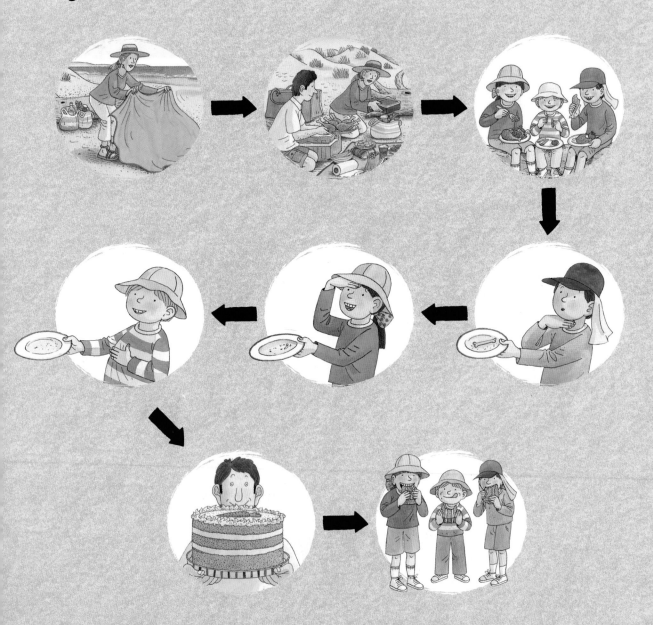

Look Back, Explorers

Where was Chip full up to?

What did Mum put on the sand?

The cake is *fantastic*. What other words can you think of for the cake?

Did you find out who ate the sandwich?

What's Next, Explorers?

Now find out how lots of picnic foods grow ...

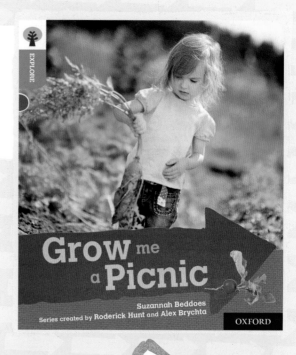

Explorer Challenge
for *Grow Me a Picnic*

What food is this part of?